You're
Doing
Great!

Cataloging-in-Publication Data is on file at the Library of Congress

Hardcover ISBN: 978-1-4019-7348-3

10 9 8 7 6 5 4 3 2 1
1st edition, October 2023

MIX
Paper | Supporting
responsible forestry
FSC
www.fsc.org
FSC® C104723

Printed in China

You're Doing Great!

Self-Care, Affirmations, and Meditations for Stressed-Out Humans

Vida Rose

HAY HOUSE, INC.

Carlsbad, California • New York City

London • Sydney • New Delhi

Thank you, Earth

CONTENTS

You made it!

we're so happy you're here

Think of this book as a rooftop garden.
It's a space where you can just exist . . .

. . . see some views . . .

. . . smell some flowers . . .

. . . and when you leave, you'll feel refreshed.

(maybe next time,
you'll bring your friends)

Throughout this book, we "helpers" will guide you through several themes of the human experience, offering creative prompts, coping skills, and contemplations to ease the ride.

You can read this book straight through or out of order. You can read it in bed or outside. You can write in it, add to the drawings, cross out things you don't like, and circle things you do like. You can dog-ear it, put your coffee cup right on top of it, or even write your own version of this book on top of this version,

because now:

this is your book.

Unless . . .
it's from the library,
of course.

In this book we're defining self-care as:

any supportive, harmless action, for the sake of

being kind to oneself now, in the present moment

I like that.

Me too.

... it takes some of the pressure off

If we accept this definition, then self-care is less about what you're doing and more about being caring

caring about how you feel!

... and then doing something about it.

Something kind.

This all sounds so easy. Do you think we really need to make a book about it?

We already did.

Do you think humans are good?

Mostly? But they live in some harmful systems.

Mmm . . .

Do you think self-care can disrupt a harmful system?

. . . it's one way to do it.

If I were a human trying to take better care of myself . . .

I would ask myself: where can I find some relief right now?

Is there some kind of freedom I'm overlooking?

Like, maybe I have more room to be wild and free that I'm taking for granted.

I would ask myself if there is some kind of peace that I can amplify.

thank you.

You would be an interesting human.

BEING HUMAN FAQ

who am I?

what do I really want?

is
this
how I look?

am I confined by
labels, boxes, and
perceptions?

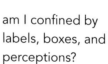

or are they building blocks for
me to do this dance on?

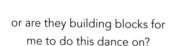

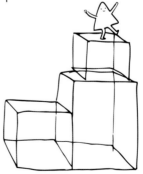

Part 1

Body Care

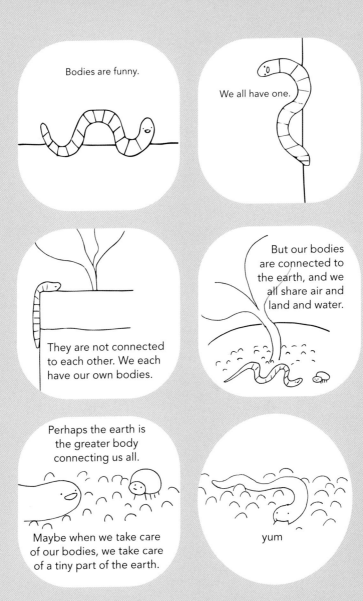

HOW TO TALK TO YOUR BODY

Most of the time we only talk about our bodies in terms of appearance or illness.

From your body's perspective, that's probably a bummer.

Here are some examples of how to talk lovingly to your body.

The idea is to have a dialogue with your body that's based in respect, the way you would treat a friend. It might feel weird at first.

try saying one (or all) of these things to your body:

"I love you, my brilliant body."

"Hello, my body, who I am learning to trust and adore."

"You are my wonderful, sensitive,

intelligent body."

"You are my spontaneously healing body."

"Body, your intelligence and power continue to amaze me. Sometimes I don't know what's going on with you, but I'm devoted to staying curious and listening to you."

"Toes are funny! You couldn't make this stuff up."

You are doing wonderful.

Now, try these out loud:

I love u legs

I love u knees

I love u bum

I love u face

I love u feet

I love u toes

I love u heart

I love u fingers

HOW TO FEEL BETTER
IN YOUR BODY RIGHT NOW

Just like your mind craves stories that stretch your imagination, your joints and muscles crave stretching through their full range of movement.

Stretching can be easy to do, I'll show you:

Go through each of your main joints one at a time.

Start with your ankles, then your knees, hips, arms, etc.

Gently explore their comfortable full range of movement.

This instantly gives relief to your joints and brings a sense of spaciousness into your body with almost no effort.

Lying down, it might look like this:

It should feel good.

but if it doesn't,
experiment with making the
movement smaller or slower, or
shifting to a different part of your body.

INSTANT MOOD BOOSTER

HOW TO GIVE YOURSELF A SHOULDER MASSAGE

gently draw circles
with your shoulders,
going forward toward
your chest

bring them up
toward your ears and
back down again

pause and
breathe,

then
switch
directions,

this time drawing circles
toward your back and
then down again to a
normal position

breathe

I'm not normal

HOW TO RELIEVE NECK TENSION

pretend I have a neck

Trace your elbow with your eyes

while you gently move it around in space.

Now do the other side.

This is a safe way of loosening and stretching your neck.

By keeping your eye on your elbow, you'll never over-extend your neck muscles.

You can also try this:

In the space in front of your face

draw circles with your nose

like this

okay I'm done!

WRIST & HAND CARE

You can give yourself a wrist and hand massage

by gently
making circles
with your wrists.

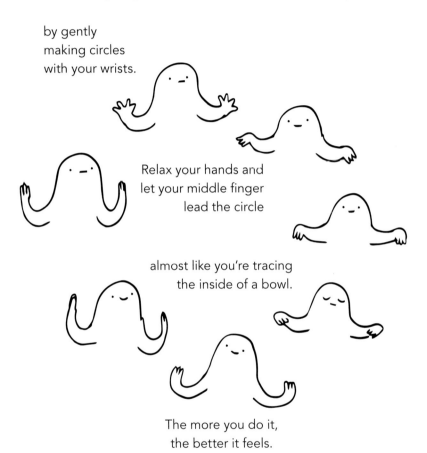

Relax your hands and
let your middle finger
lead the circle

almost like you're tracing
the inside of a bowl.

The more you do it,
the better it feels.

HOW TO BE KIND TO
YOUR HIPS AND SPINE

Find a comfortable position lying
on your back with your knees up.

Gently rock your knees
from side to side.

Notice the subtle ways the
movement takes pressure
off your back.

YOGA FOR PEOPLE WHO DON'T WANT TO GET UP

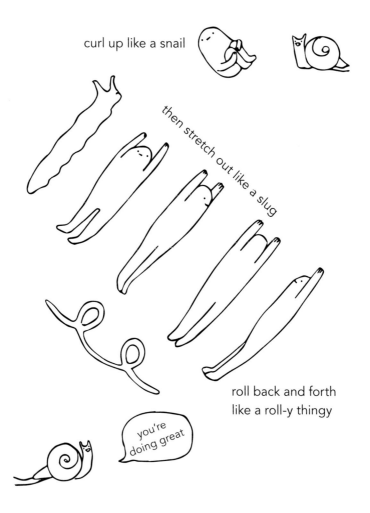

MORE SPINE LOVE

If it's comfortable for you, lie on your back with your arms and legs up. (Well, up-ish)

Shake, wiggle, make a weird sound

Play with your comfortable full range of movement, and then

relax

btw, if lying on the floor doesn't work for you,

you can get the same benefit by wiggling in your chair

or leaning on it

I love you

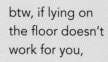

or leaning on the wall or doorframe.

HOW TO HOLD YOURSELF

You can give yourself endorphins by hugging yourself.

Experiment with different ways of wrapping your arms around yourself. Give yourself a good squeeze.

Breathe, and take a moment to enjoy your own hug.

Kiss your arm

Kiss your hand

yay

DEEP BREATH BREAK

start here: follow the line with your finger and breathe in…

in…

and hold for 2 seconds

and breathe out…

wonderful

ah

all the way out

HOW TO BE NICE TO YOUR KNEES

This sounds weird, but scoot your bum against a wall, like this.

Then swing your legs up, like this.

You can stay like this for 1–10 minutes.

Listen to your body.

It should feel relaxing,

but if it doesn't,

try wiggling and adjusting your legs.

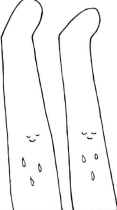

Having your legs go against gravity gives your knees a break and allows lymphatic fluids to drain.

Also, btw:

If legs up a wall isn't accessible to you, here are some variations you can try:

halfway up

legs lounging on a pile of pillows

pillows smooshed against the wall to make a leg ramp

you're amazing

REMEMBER TO DRINK WATER

make friends with water

ask your water where it came from
and learn about the watersheds near you

SPEAK KIND WORDS
INTO YOUR WATER

Water takes the shape of its container.

Words are containers too.

Here are some kind words you can offer your water:

Thank you for coming to me, water.

You are wonderful, water.

I love you

glug glug

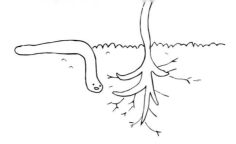

BODY CARE AFFIRMATIONS

Try saying these out loud or to yourself:

Wow, it's an honor to be alive and be in a body

I'm remembering that my
body is an experience,
not an object

I'm ready to listen to my body and show
it all the kindness I can muster, even if I
look weird while I do it

I'm relearning how to do
what feels good for my body

I love my body and I love the earth

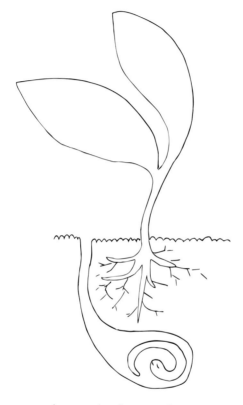

okay, my body is tired now.

let's rest, body

Part 2

Emotional
Care

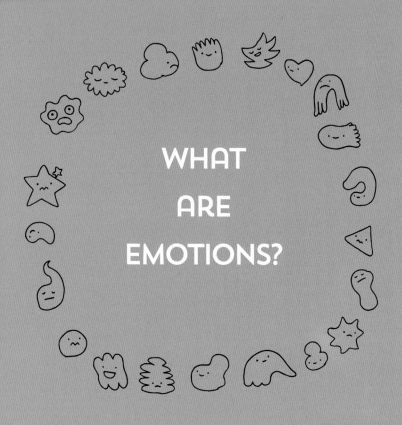

WHAT
ARE
EMOTIONS?

Sometimes in the moment,
they can feel like entire universes
with no end.

Intense emotions can feel destabilizing.

One way to see emotions is as energies passing through you.

Only you can decide how to make sense of the information they bring.

In a way, emotions are like
a secret language between
you and the universe—

which is kind of exciting,

because
you're alive,
the universe is
talking to you,

and you can feel things!

But also, sometimes those things
you feel suck, and it's hard.

This part of the book has helpful tips
for moving through emotions.

SELF-CARE TECHNIQUE #1:
WATERFALL

This is a good technique for soothing intense emotions that are outside of your every-day experience, like nerves around a performance or a conflict with a friend.

When you feel safe and alone (like in bed), let the emotions know you are ready to feel them, and imagine them washing over you, like a waterfall.

You can remind yourself that you're totally safe to feel whatever comes up.

breathe

After a few minutes of intentionally feeling,
you'll notice the intensity of the emotions fade.

Note: If you're someone who has a hard time
getting to sleep, don't try this right before
bed, since it might make your mind too
excited. Try it early in the morning instead.

SELF-CARE TECHNIQUE #2: MERIDIAN TAPPING

Sometimes emotions can become stuck in the body.

You can tell something is off because your breathing has changed, your body is tense, or you may even feel like you're not in your body at all.

Tapping is a wonderful tool for both verbal process-ing and moving emotions through your body.

Meridian tapping—sometimes called the Emotional Freedom Technique (or EFT)—is a modality that draws on the mapping of energy meridians in traditional Chinese medicine and from positive psychology.

Basically, you tap on specific energy points on your body while talking through your emotions. This soothes your nervous system and helps your body release tension.

Here's how to get started:

1. Choose an emotion to focus on for each tapping session. If you are overwhelmed or can't differentiate between your emotions, lump them into a category that makes sense to you. For example, lots of emotions fit into "fear," or if you have synesthesia, you might say "yellow" or whatever color/image/sensation represents your emotions best at the moment.

2. Rate your current emotional state on a scale of 1–10, 1 being living your best life, and 10 being in the midst of a panic attack. This can help you check your progress later.

3. Using 2–3 fingers, tap repetitively on each of the points shown on the next page, as if you are an annoying customer ringing a concierge bell. Your tap should be gentle, but with enough strength that you can feel it. It should be enough pressure to get your attention, but tapping should never ever ever ever ever hurt.

4. Watch tapping videos. There are thousands of tapping videos online, and every practitioner has a different style. Find out what works for you. (Btw, it's very normal that you might cry, yawn, sneeze, or even burp as the energy moves through your body!)

Promise you won't just read this without tapping —you have to tap!

Wow, I'm really feeling stressed!

(name your emotion)

It makes sense that I'm feeling stressed…look at all these reasons.

(validate your emotion)

I'm feeling so much pressure and tension right now, and it's so stressful.

(elaborate on your emotion)

under nose/above lip

And even though I'm feeling like the stress–mayor of Stress–Town, USA…

(make fun of yourself a tiny bit)

below lip/above chin

…I still accept myself exactly as I am right now, because I'm the best, most charming, and adorable stress–monster who ever stressed, and I one-million-percent love myself.

(declare self-acceptance and love)

under clavicle

I've probably stressed this stress as far as I can stress it…and I'm ready to make a change. I really want to feel some relief. So I'm choosing to release this stress, and I'm taking my foot off the stress pedal.

(declare that you are choosing to shift)

under armpit

I am choosing to feel relief now. I'm choosing to breathe deeper, to feel as good as I possibly can right now, and to take some pressure off of myself.

(reiterate your transformation as well as your self-acceptance)

Check in with your stress rating. Did it go down?

If you still feel high levels of stress, try repeating the round again.

Here's a picture of all the tapping points:

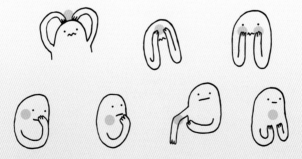

…that was a lot of information.

Phew! Let's take a deep

breathing break:

in..

follow the flight path with your
finger and take a deep breath

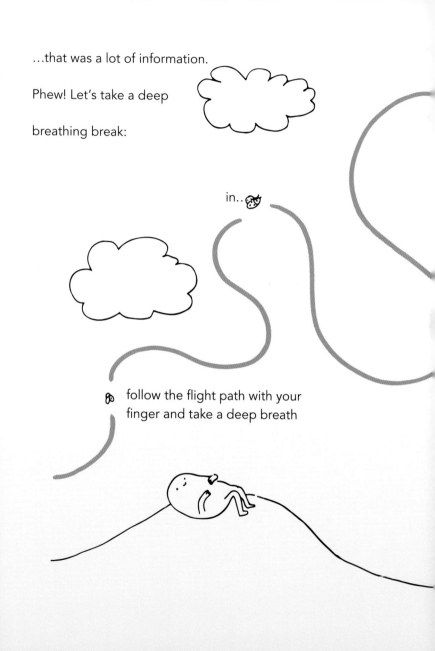

hold at the top

and out...

wonderful

When You Just Need to Talk Sh*t

Sometimes we just need to just say what's on our minds, and it can be healthy to get it out there and share our feelings with someone else. Some people call it "venting," like opening a window.

Venting can sometimes be scary. In a better, more evolved world, there might be private truth-speaking booths in buildings, the way that there are public bathrooms, accompanied by a general understanding that some sentiments are for the sake of expression only and are not meant to be taken personally.

Until then, here are some ideas for venting in a way that feels safe. First of all:

ask for consent when you vent

I have so much going on right now that I need to let out some steam. Do you have capacity to listen to me vent for like five minutes?

How to Talk Sh*t When Nobody Wants to Listen

If you are unable to find someone who has the capacity to listen to you vent, here's something you can do:

set a timer for 5 to 10 minutes

open the voice recording app on your phone.

Say everything that is on your mind—everything you want to get out of your system. It's okay to be mean! Having it recorded makes it feel like someone is listening, even if it's just you being your own best friend.

You can either keep your recording private or delete it if you want.

By creating a venting container like this, you can safely express yourself without wearing yourself down or bringing this energy into other areas of your life.

thank you
for listening

Emotional Care Affirmations

Affirmations are like planting seeds for kinder thought patterns. The most effective way to use them is to write them down and put them somewhere you'll organically see them from time to time, like your phone wallpaper or on the wall next to your bed. Read them matter-of-factly when you're in a good mood, and read them gently if you need a little more tenderness. Below are some example affirmations:

Feeling emotions takes courage.
I'm sensitive because I'm brave.

I love knowing how I really feel.

My emotions are just tourists.
I don't have to worry about
them staying forever.

I'm learning to take responsibility
for my emotion's okay-ness.
I'm pretty good at it.

What Can Support You Right Now?

Sometimes a tiny action can bring great relief. Below are some simple and helpful ideas. What actions would you add?

self hug

doing nothing

fresh air

the bathroom

doing something creative

drinking water

your bed

sammich

being in nature

making a list

texting a friend

u r wonderful

Dreaming Beyond Worry

Write or draw your daydreams in the clouds below. What kind of change and growth do you hope for?

Amazing!

Wow! Your brain is excellent.

You should write a whole book.

A
MESSAGE
FROM THE
HELPERS

We know that every human being experiences a wide range of feelings, but within the systems in which humans live, these feelings are not always accepted. There is often rejection of emotional expression, whether it is grief or joy or something in between.

Sometimes, others perceive the full rainbow of emotions as a threat, because its complexity and power can't be controlled. When this happens, humans can't learn how to feel and express themselves in healthy, safe ways.

We want you to know that your emotions are completely yours—they exist for you. It's an honor to be alive and feel things, and it's temporary. Embrace it!

The more you can learn to feel without fear, the less afraid you will be of others.

You humans have so much more in common than you think you do.

We are rooting for you!

Part 3

Energy and Spirit Care

A MESSAGE FROM A PEACEFUL SPIRIT IN THE GARDEN OF LIFE

In ways
big...

...and small.

I work to attract beneficial visitors to the garden.

LIKE YOU

I think who I am and what I do are pretty great.

Being me is my favorite.

I know that for humans, being who you really are is a little more complicated.

In the human world, there are a lot of roles to play and work to do that you don't even get to decide for yourself. It makes it harder to stay in balance and remember who you are.

That's why this next part of the book is all about taking care of your energy and your spirit.

HOW TO MEDITATE

One way to think about meditation is: sitting in goodwill toward yourself.

If that sounds hard to accomplish, try thinking about your best friend, a pet you love, or just anyone you really super like.

Feel, in your own body, how you feel toward them.

As you do so, notice your breathing – how it goes in, the point where it switches from inhale to exhale – and how it goes out.

Now you're meditating.

FRIEND CONSTELLATION MEDITATION

Humans look at maps a lot. They often see arbitrary borders, town and city names, and car-centric orientation designed to get someone from point A to point B efficiently.

In this meditation, you'll create a totally subjective friend constellation map, with you at the center.

This is a radical way to orient yourself in the world according to what you value, and it is a great way to feel connected to people who are far away in distance, but near to your heart. It also nourishes your imagination and your relationship to the earth.

Ready to get started?

Think about a friend you love who is far away.

Imagine them sitting in their home

and imagine yourself doing the same thing.

Imagine a sparkly, magic thread of positive energy that connects you and your friend.
(It can be any color you like.)

Now think of all the space and land and water that is between the two of you.

Imagine that sparkly thread traveling across the land,

across water,

across buildings and cars and things.

Imagine the people and animals it passes and what they are doing.

Imagine the trees and how the light may be hitting them.

Is there a nice breeze blowing?

Imagine that sparkly thread creating a constellation of goodwill that sparks joy and brings benefits to everyone who crosses its path.

You can make a friend constellation map with as many friends as you want!

WHAT'S UP WITH YOUR ENERGY?

There are many things shaping how you experience your own energy right now, including:

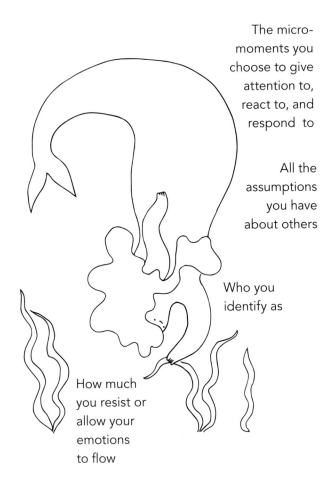

The micro-moments you choose to give attention to, react to, and respond to

All the assumptions you have about others

Who you identify as

How much you resist or allow your emotions to flow

How to Feel Your Own Energy

Become curious about what makes you authentically happy. Keep a running list of your happiest moments. Be honest with yourself.

You'll notice patterns: what you were doing, who you were with,

if you were at the beach or in the mountains,

if you were learning a new skill or volunteering to help people or spending time with family,

or being alone and resting

These are the things that make you feel the most like you. Every once in a while, peek at your list and ask yourself if you have space to be more yourself.

How to Protect Your Energy

If you're a human and you're about to go into a city or log on to social media (anywhere there is a lot of people, commotion, and energy),

you will experience: people doing their best, braving this life with grace,

being kind and considerate to strangers, and living in the peaceful chaos that life breathes when it has space and diversity. The world is varied, wild, and wonderful...

... but some scary things exist too.

It's good to have energetic protection tools.

None of them are one size fits all, and there is nuance in any given situation.

The point is to have a fun life. Give yourself permission to be playful and imaginative, even if you're in self-preservation mode. Enjoying your life is your birthright.

The following techniques are like energetic versions of affirmations: they plant supportive seeds that grow along with you.

ENERGY PROTECTION TECHNIQUE #1:

Look for What You Want to See

As you're leaving your house for the day, take a deep breath and think of something you want to notice while you're out.

As you step out into the world, consciously take note of the beauty that you see.

maybe a cool tree, a delightful dog, or just a funny, random thing.

Being in touch with the beauty and humor of the world is a form of psychic protection.

ENERGY PROTECTION TECHNIQUE #2:

Friend Appreciation

 Take a deep breath and think of a friend you love and the kind of day you wish for them:

creative joy, bills paid, really good lunch, etc.

Tune in to the feelings that you want them to experience.

The good energy you send to your friend will bounce back and boost your aura.

HOW TO CLEAR YOUR ENERGY

The world of human emotions has a lot of momentum and variety in it, which is beautiful. It allows you to feel alive, be creative, and experience new things. A side effect of this world is that sometimes it's possible to accumulate (really quickly) a kind of energy that doesn't feel good to you.

If this happens, don't freak out. And don't worry about where the energy came from—it can be a chicken-and-egg conundrum when it comes to vibes. Was it a projection? Was it someone else's fault? It doesn't matter. Just focus on bringing yourself back to a baseline that is more authentically you.

Here are some ideas for clearing energy garbage:

hum or
sing it away
with a song

shake it off by
shaking your body

(if you're in public and you don't
wanna draw attention to yourself,
find a bathroom to shake in)

wash it off

or, if you're
in a pinch…

HOW TO PRAY

(Even if You Aren't Religious)

Prayer is just about tuning in to what you want to happen instead of letting the narrative of worry play on repeat.

You can pray to: the force of love, the magic of nature, the mystery of reality, or the higher power of your choice.

Even if you don't believe in any kind of divine intelligence, you can still benefit from praying, and achieve a soothed nervous system and more positive thinking.

Here is a simple prayer to try:

(Feel free to adjust this to your personal beliefs as needed.)

Universe, friendly forces, helpers
I'm putting in a request for the best
 possible outcome for _____
(person, situation you're worried about).

I really want it to go like _____
(outcome you want) or something even
better than I can fathom.

Thank you for listening.

I love you.

Part 4

Creativity and Mental Health Care

How would you define "mental health"?
If we were humans, we would really think about that. From our perspective, humans thrive best when they have supportive systems (externally and internally) that allow them to be comfortably and playfully in touch with the beauty and absurdity of reality. In order to have playfulness, beauty, and absurdity, a human has to have all of their basic needs met: shelter, food, and medicine. These are human rights!

It's kind of exciting how the earth (biologically) and the world (figuratively) are in a constant ongoing process of creation and destruction.

So are you – because you are a part of it all.

we think you're pretty cool

WHAT IS ART?

Speaking of the ongoing
process of creation and
destruction, let's talk
about art.

Art is following a feeling

until it becomes a sharable experience.

 When we experience art,
we empathize and we change.

CREATIVE MANIFESTO
STARTER PACK

There is an artist in everyone. What kind of artist are you? This is a template to help you explore your creative identity. Your identity can change over time. Come back to this exercise whenever you want some creative inspiration.

In life, I really value . . . .

. . . .

I love when . . . .

. . . .
happens in a story.

I love when music makes me feel . . . .

. . . .

I would love to see more stories about . . . .

. . . .

The most grandiose vision I have for myself as a creator is . . . .

. . . .

A running list of friends, family, and peers and the traits I admire in them:

UNDERRATED CREATIVITY AND MENTAL HEALTH SUPPORTS

1. Feeling safe and cared for

2. Letting yourself feel bored

3. Taking walks with
no destination

What would you add to this list?

BOOST YOUR CREATIVITY BY LISTENING TO BIRTH STORIES

Listening to people's birth stories is a powerful way to connect to your humanity. Before you can be creative, you have to be human.

Every single human you know was born. Isn't that wild to think about?

Birth can be both a visceral and direct metaphor for the creative process. Over time, integrating birth stories into your imagination and understanding of the world can help you to be more present as a creator.

Just like no two creative endeavors are the same, every birth story is unique. But the themes are often the same: excitement, feelings of connection, wonderment, fear, and pain. The honor of being alive and being a part of creation happens in real time during birth.

Learn about the mysteries and realities of childbirth and deepen your creative soul.

(Remember to get consent before asking for these details.)

DEEP BREATH BREAK

Let's take a moment to relax.

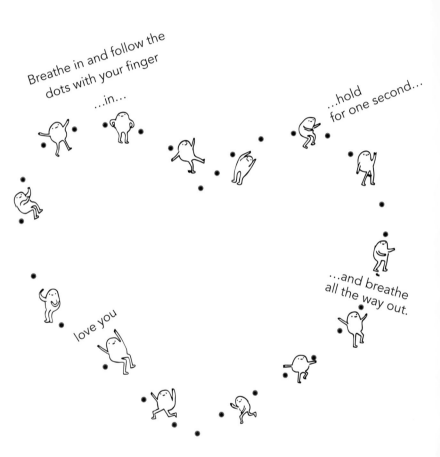

Breathe in and follow the dots with your finger

…in…

…hold for one second…

…and breathe all the way out.

love you

HOW TO HEAL YOUR IMAGINATION

Does your imagination need healing?

From a young age, you've likely been confronted with imagery and ideas with the purpose of making you a better consumer and a well-behaved citizen. Think sneaky advertising, celebrity culture, divisive rhetoric, etc. The genius of propaganda is that it comes off as natural. As if it just... belongs there.

And just like that, your ideas of what is possible can become hijacked by something that doesn't benefit you or anyone you love. Your imagination is the raw material of life, the place where ideas become reality, and it is important to reclaim your creative capacity.

Human imaginations are all connected into a collective imagination: the things you believe to be possible have the potential to change your life, the lives of others - even the whole world!

Here is the good news: you can heal your imagination and reconnect with your creativity and your truth.

Here are some tips to get you started:

Write down a list of the most enchanting books, movies, or albums you've ever experienced.
What are the common threads?

Ask your inner child what kind of stories they want to explore.

Seek out art made by people whose lives are very different from your own.

Be pickier about the stories you consume.

Your attention will breathe life into a story. Ask yourself if this is a story you want to breathe life into.

It's okay to want to just be entertained sometimes, but entertainment never exists in a vacuum.

When you tell the story of who you are
and how the world is,

through art or just casual conversation,

leave space for the
miracles you crave.

Make room for
a redemption arc
or some other
unexpected...

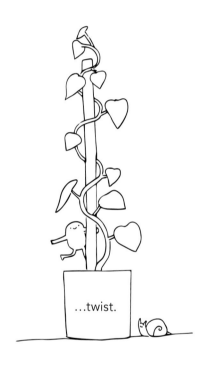

...twist.

A QUICK AND EASY MEDITATION

You are made of
mostly water.

Imagine a lake in
your mind.

Every time you
breathe in and
out, the water
becomes calmer.

Breathe in: imag-
ine how the sun-
light reflects on the
calm water.

Breathe out: imagine a
tiny fish swimming by.

Water is life.

CREATIVITY AND MENTAL HEALTH AFFIRMATIONS

Here are affirmations to support creative growth and mental well-being. Read these after meditating, before working, or anytime you need a break.

I'm learning to prioritize my truest joy.

Every day I find moments to unwind and relax.

I love to listen deeply.

I'm really good at being my own cheerleader.

Every day I find evidence that I am safe.

I let myself make art, even if I don't understand it.

Creative community is all around me.

Part 5

Transitions and Self-Care

Hey, human friend.

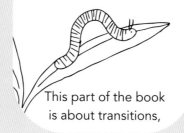

This part of the book
is about transitions,

the in-between stages in life.

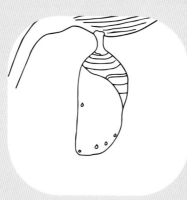

They can be really challenging.

Most humans only pick up a book like this if they're going through a transition of their own.

Maybe you've outgrown something, internally or externally, or maybe you've experienced a move, a breakup, a loss of a loved one, or a coming out.

Whether you're here in a spirit of openness, or in need of a leap of faith, we appreciate you and we believe in you.

SOME SENSATIONS YOU MIGHT FEEL DURING TIMES OF TRANSITION

a lack of definition

transparency

grayness

spaciness

anxiety

wiggliness

ups and downs

fear

grief

OTHER SENSATIONS YOU MIGHT FEEL DURING TIMES OF TRANSITION

confidence

gratitude

happiness

and even

being 100 percent okay

All of these sensations
are okay to feel.

Unwanted change can come with grief and
wanted change can come with joy. Sometimes
there's no linear logic to the felt experience of life.

But how amazing is it that…

You're Alive!

YOU'RE ALIVE AND WE LOVE YOU

Thank you for being alive and thank you for reading this book.

Thank you for being you: never finished, always changing, perfectly human you.

On the next page you'll find some self-care ideas for moving through transitional phases.

(These are all easy and don't require you to buy anything.)

BREATHE

When life feels overwhelming, the most important thing to do is just breathe.

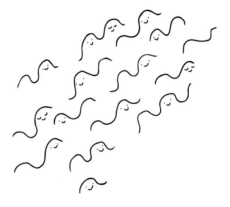

Imagine that the air molecules around you are friendly, and if you breathe slowly and intentionally, they can really help you.

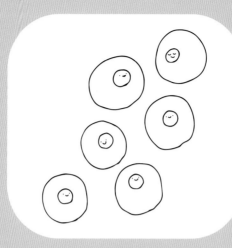

Oxygen makes friends with
your red blood cells

and that helps your brain
and your body feel good.

Thank you,
air.

BE KIND TO THE MIRROR PERSON

For most humans, when you look in the mirror, you see only what you don't like about your physical appearance. You can't see the whole person you really are with the same compassion you might extend to a friend.

During transitional times, you can feel more sensitive and vulnerable.

While you're in an uncertain space, you have an opportunity to grow compassion for the person you see in the mirror.

Here is a starter dialogue for making peace with your reflection:

Hi, I see you.

I love you just how you are right now,

and even though talking like this feels awkward,

I'm on your team and I love you.

TAKE A WALK

it doesn't have to be far

cheer on the
signs of life

this is all new!

pretend
you're on vacation

look at the sky

it's big

when you return, you'll be refreshed

See how good you are at transitions?

HOW TO REFRAME ANXIETY

It's normal to experience high anxiety during a transitional period.

Maybe it feels like your mind is racing with "what ifs," or maybe it's just an unsettling feeling, like there is an alarm you can't turn off. Acknowledge that this is something you're experiencing. Your feelings are valid, and they will also change.

Anxiety is not an identity or a permanent state, even if it seems like it's been with you for so long. Moments of relief and inner peace can be cultivated. Like any good habit, they take practice.

The next pages include affirmations and practices to help you reframe your anxiety, so that you can choose what it means.

This can help put some wiggle room and breathing space between you, your emotional experience, and your glorious, fantastic imagination.

Affirmations to Reframe Anxiety

Maybe this anxious sensation
means that I care about life and
I'm excited to be alive.
I like that.

Maybe I'm feeling this much because I care so
deeply about what happens. I'm a caring person.

I love that I have such a vivid imagination.
Maybe I'll write a book!

I really love the people I love,
and I want us to all be okay.
That's the kind of person I am.

SOOTHING MEDITATION

Count Backward and Breathe

This is a good place to start if you don't already have a meditation practice, or a coping skill for heightened states of emotion.

There's only one you!

REMEMBER TO REST

You don't have to do stuff all the time. Sometimes, you can just rest.

It seems like it would be easy, but it can be challenging to let yourselves rest when you need to. If you're in a new routine or facing big life changes, you are using more energy than you normally do, and you need to rest more to make up for it.

Humans are all conditioned to believe that their self-worth is dependent on their productivity, and some of them have additional layers of conditioning that make rest challenging. Look at your environment, your culture, and the habits of the people who raised you. Were you taught that rest is laziness?

Resting can sometimes feel scary and unnatural. If fear comes up when you want to take a break or a nap or a retreat, know that fear is not who you are.

Ask your body how much rest it needs right now and treat it with kindness.

YOUR PACE IS YOURS

Often when humans are going through a big change, they just want to hurry up and adapt. Sometimes it happens that way. Other times, you experience changes gradually,

fading in and out of identities so slowly you can't really see it. Your style of navigating changes might be mirrored in the way that you literally move through the world.

What are you like when you're strolling through a park?

Driving through a city you've never been in before?

Stepping inside your favorite bookstore?

How do you like to travel through space and time? Does acknowledging your travel style offer you a more compassionate view of your growth?

AFFIRMATION FOR RIDING UNCERTAIN WAVES

Use these affirmations to give your-self extra kindness and hope during life changes. Put them somewhere you will see throughout the day— maybe on your phone or written as a note near your desk.

Teeny-tiny things I can't even see are going right for me right now.

By the time I notice the poo-poo pile, help is on the way. I will look for the helpers.

Since all humans are the same amount of human, and everyone is completely unique, I am only ever in competition with myself.

I'm open to the best possible outcome... even if I have no idea what that would be.

I'm right on time.

HOW TO CREATE INNER SPACE

a little patch of sky through a window,

Look for something beautiful in nature, whether it's a sunset,

or a tiny leaf.

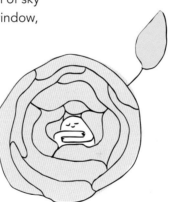

Close your eyes and breathe it in.

Imagine it's a part of you now.

HOW TO CREATE YOUR OWN INNER SANCTUARY

You can put anything you want in here: stars, palm trees, mountains.

Close your eyes and go through the five senses of your inner sanctuary:

What colors do you see?

What does it smell like?

How does the air feel on your skin?

Imagine munching on a snack you love.

What does it taste like?

What do you hear?

you're doing great

Part 6

Forgiveness and Self-Care

Forgiveness is a gift you can give to yourself.

It's not about saying that what happened was okay.

It's about accepting a past event and taking your energy back from it. If you are in a rut in any area of your life, consider starting a forgiveness practice. This part of the book is about approaching forgiveness with creativity.

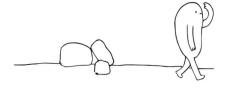

If you're not ready to forgive someone, you can forgive:

a situation

the universe

reality

your higher power

yourself

*If you are presently being mistreated or abused, do not use this tool. Seek support to leave the situation. After you establish safety, then you can decide if you're ready to forgive.

HOW TO BUILD YOUR FORGIVENESS MUSCLE

The bigger the misstep you are forgiving, the longer of a process it might be. Don't try to jump in and forgive your worst childhood traumas right away.

Practice giving grace to yourself in small ways: being patient while you learn a new thing, speaking kindly to yourself when you make a mistake, accepting your emotions as they come up:

Humans often hold the worst grudges against themselves. You're doing your best. Remember how tiny your mistakes are in the grand scheme of human blunders!

HOW TO PROTECT YOUR PEACE

Often resentment builds because someone has sacrificed something they deeply care for, like quality friend time, sleeping in, or going to shows.

The better you know your authentic joy—your preferred pace, kind of peace, how you like to feel, what you value— the easier it is to make supportive boundaries.

The next pages have fill-in-the-blank worksheets to help you understand YOUR definition of peace.

FILL IN THE BLANKS

The last time I experienced true **FUN**, I was with

_____, and I was _____.

In my body, I felt _____.

At the heart of my **FUN** is _____.

The last time I experienced true **BLISS**, I was with

_____, and I was _____.

In my body, I felt _____.

At the heart of my **BLISS** is _____.

The last time I experienced true **SWEETNESS**, I was with

_____, and I was _____.

In my body, I felt _____.

At the heart of my **SWEETNESS** is _____.

The last time I experienced true **LOVE**, I was with

_____, and I was _____.

In my body, I felt _____.

At the heart of my **LOVE**, is _____.

DEEP BREATH BREAK

and breathe out

hold for one second

START HERE!! follow the flight path
with your finger
and breathe in

FORGIVENESS PROMPT

Make It a Monster

If you are feeling resentful about something that happened, imagine the situation/person/event as a monster.

What kind of monster would it be? What would it look like? Would it have scales or fur? Would it breathe fire or swim in sewers?
Draw or write about your monster in as much detail as possible.

Here are some resentment monster
ideas to get you started:

Student Loan
Debt Monster

Bad Lighting
Monster

Fossil Fuel
Worship Monster

After you've fleshed out your monster, it's time to talk to it. Either in writing or out loud, tell your monster exactly how you feel about it.

Speak your truth until you feel relief in your chest.

Then, ask yourself if you are ready to forgive, and if you are, say, "I forgive you"

until you feel lighter.

HOW TO APOLOGIZE

When You F*cked Up

You're human, it happens! This simple guide will help.

1. Be specific and straightforward.

"I'm sorry I used your toothbrush."

2. Acknowledge the impact of your harm, and say what you wish you'd done differently.

"I can see you are truly disgusted. I wish I had asked you first."

3. Make a commitment to change your behavior going forward.

"From now on, I will only use my own toothbrush. Can I buy you a new one?"

IMAGINARY APOLOGY

Visualization

When it's possible, ask for an apology. But sometimes, for whatever reason, a person is not available to give an apology. The next few pages have a visualization to try if you are still craving one.

Take a moment—in a safe, uninterrupted space—to imagine the apology you want to hear. What are the exact words you are wanting? You can write them down, or just think them in your head.

Focus on the underlying feeling of the apology.

What kind of attention are you wanting to receive?

Tune in to it and allow yourself to feel it in your body.

Allow yourself to be nourished.

Breathe.

Whatever peace you can imagine you deserve, you do.

Your relationship with the offending person might not change, but you can learn what it is that you need.

your heart
is good

Part 7

Love and Joy Care

Do you think you have to love yourself
before you can love others?

Or do you think you should focus on loving
others as much as you can and not worry about
yourself as much?

Does it matter?

Maybe not!

Loving is good

Go love!

Love is Natural and Normal and Real

It doesn't have to be a special thing that only happens with romantic partners or family.

You love a lot more people than you think you do, and more people love you than you know.

Love has many branches, like this tree.

I'm alive and you're alive at the same time –
and I love you!

HOW TO KEEP IN TOUCH WITH LOVE

Keep an ongoing list of non-couple, nontraditional loves.

Couple love can be beautiful, but when a society values it above other kinds of love, like love for friends, nature, or ideas, everyone misses out. Humans need to experience more love, and the love is all around them.

Here are some ideas:

tree love

helper love

water love

art love

(this is a mirror. you're the art.)

I love this moment

and I love you

LOVE MEDITATION

Think of someone you love – whoever comes to your mind first.

Imagine them first as a baby, and then growing older as they move through time. See them resilient and full of life, pushing through challenges, and waiting in hopefulness.

See them grow, change, work, make choices, and survive—all the way up until their present age.

Then imagine them walking toward you with a big bouquet of love. They went through so much to bring you this love. And you are worth it.

Take a moment to breathe and receive and feel the love. Know that letting yourself feel their love is healing to both of you.

WHAT IS JOY?

Sometimes people use the words "happiness" and "joy" interchangeably.

This is one way to differentiate between the two:

Happiness is conditional, as in:

I have this thing now, so I'm happy.

Joy is spontaneous, as in:

For no reason, I'm suddenly delighted.

HOW TO BOOST YOUR JOY

(The Sunshine Dance)

Here is a simple dance move to release tension from your neck and shoulders and to bring energy to your heart space. It's called The Sunshine. Put on a song you love and try it out.

Basically, you are the sun

and your hands and arms

are tracing the rays

that shine out from you

in a motion that's similar to swimming.

Breathe!

Feel how the tension dissipates

from your body.

You are so bright and so loved.

4 WAYS TO LOVE YOURSELF

1. Quit something you hate doing

2. Take longer doing something you love

3. Make choices in your own time

4. Let yourself change your mind

LOVE AND JOY AFFIRMATIONS

Try saying these out loud or in your mind.

Joy is in my nature.

I can tune in to love or joy whenever I want to.

I'm loved because I'm alive.

I'm made of love.

Tune In to

Kindness

With this book, we, the helpers, tried to use love and cuteness to trick you into seeing how loveable and cute you are.

We were trying to sneak you over to the receiving end of your own kindness.

...did it work?

Everything grows in tiny increments, including our own personal development. Most humans aren't taught to honor that enough.

At the end of the day,
every tool we teach exists to help you

appreciate where you are,

reach a slightly more expansive view,

and bring some relief – or maybe even upliftment.

All of this
is in service to a greater joy and love.

Our hope for you is that you can wake up to fun and playfulness that nature and other humans are putting out all around
you, all the time.

We are the helpers. We hang out in the liminal spaces:
between you and other humans, between different versions
of you, between seasons and growth spurts and moods.

We are always ready to be curious and kind, and you can
tune in to us whenever you want.

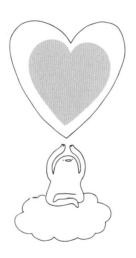

ACKNOWLEDGMENTS

This book was made possible by so much encouragement and generosity. A huge thank you to my family for their patience and love during this process. Thank you to my creative communities, online and irl, for nurturing this work from the beginning. Thank you to everyone who reached out asking if I would write a book: I did it! Deep gratitude to my Patreon supporters for believing in me. A huge thank you to the team at Hay House for making this dream a reality. So much love to the creatives and healers everywhere who build their stages out of the boxes they could'nt fit into. To all of the helpers—in the visible and invisible world—thank you for holding it all together. I love you all.

AUTHOR BIO

Vida Rose is an artist, educator, and a heart-eyes-emoji in human form living in Seattle, Washington. Her creative comics encourage self-care, peace, and intentional reshaping of the harmful systems around us into something beautiful. In addition to creating her artwork, Vida likes to lucid dream, belly dance, and love. She mostly keeps her house plants alive.

You can find Vida on Instagram and TikTok: @comics_and_selfcare.

We hope you enjoyed this Hay House book. If you'd like to receive our online catalog featuring additional information on Hay House books and products, or if you'd like to find out more about the Hay Foundation, please contact:

Hay House, Inc., P.O. Box 5100, Carlsbad, CA 92018-5100
(760) 431-7695 or (800) 654-5126
(760) 431-6948 (fax) or (800) 650-5115 (fax)
www.hayhouse.com® • www.hayfoundation.org

———

Published in Australia by: Hay House Australia Pty. Ltd.,
18/36 Ralph St., Alexandria NSW 2015
Phone: 612-9669-4299 • *Fax:* 612-9669-4144
www.hayhouse.com.au

Published in the United Kingdom by: Hay House UK, Ltd.,
The Sixth Floor, Watson House, 54 Baker Street, London W1U 7BU
Phone: +44 (0)20 3927 7290 • *Fax:* +44 (0)20 3927 7291
www.hayhouse.co.uk

Published in India by: Hay House Publishers India,
Muskaan Complex, Plot No. 3, B-2, Vasant Kunj, New Delhi 110 070
Phone: 91-11-4176-1620 • *Fax:* 91-11-4176-1630
www.hayhouse.co.in

———

Access New Knowledge.
Anytime. Anywhere.

Learn and evolve at your own pace
with the world's leading experts.

www.hayhouseU.com

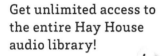

Hay House Podcasts
Bring Fresh, Free Inspiration Each Week!

Hay House proudly offers a selection of life-changing audio content via our most popular podcasts!

Hay House Meditations Podcast

Features your favorite Hay House authors guiding you through meditations designed to help you relax and rejuvenate. Take their words into your soul and cruise through the week!

Dr. Wayne W. Dyer Podcast

Discover the timeless wisdom of Dr. Wayne W. Dyer, world-renowned spiritual teacher and affectionately known as "the father of motivation." Each week brings some of the best selections from the 10-year span of Dr. Dyer's talk show on Hay House Radio.

Hay House Podcast

Enjoy a selection of insightful and inspiring lectures from Hay House Live events, listen to some of the best moments from previous Hay House Radio episodes, and tune in for exclusive interviews and behind-the-scenes audio segments featuring leading experts in the fields of alternative health, self-development, intuitive medicine, success, and more! Get motivated to live your best life possible by subscribing to the free Hay House Podcast.

Find Hay House podcasts on iTunes, or visit
www.HayHouse.com/podcasts for more info.